Flying
Machines

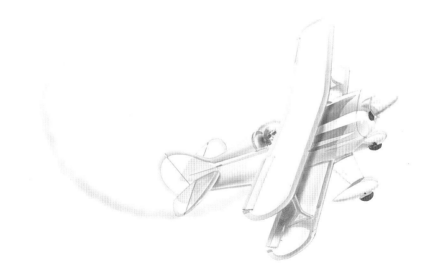

Angela Royston

Illustrated by
Sebastian Quigley

Heinemann

Contents

First published in Great Britain in 1997 by Heinemann Children's Reference,
an imprint of Heinemann Educational Publishers, Halley Court, Jordan Hill, Oxford, OX2 8EJ,
a division of Reed Educational & Professional Publishing Ltd.

MADRID ATHENS PRAGUE WARSAW FLORENCE PORTSMOUTH NH
CHICAGO SAO PAULO SINGAPORE TOKYO MEXICO MELBOURNE
AUCKLAND IBADAN GABORONE JOHANNESBURG KAMPALA NAIROBI

© Reed Educational & Professional Publishing Ltd, 1997

ISBN 0 431 06541 1

British Library Cataloguing in Publication Data
Royston, Angela, First look through flying machines
1. Airplanes - Juvenile literature
I. Title II. Flying machines 629.1'333

Photo credits: page 7, 11, 12 (centre right) and 18: © Austin J Brown;
page 8: Tony Stone Images © David Ximeno Tejada; page 12 (bottom left): © Britstock-IFA Ltd;
page 23 (top right): © US Air Force; page 23 (bottom right): © TRH/R Winslade.

Editor: Alyson Jones
Designer: Peter Clayman
Picture Researcher: Liz Eddison
Art Director: Cathy Tincknell
Production Controller: Lorraine Stebbing

Printed and bound in Italy.
See-through pages printed by SMIC, France.

Flying for Fun

Most flying machines carry passengers or things from place to place, but some people fly gliders and hang-gliders just for fun. Gliders have no engines. They float gently on the wind.

Hang-gliders are launched into the air from the top of a steep slope or cliff. The pilots steer by moving their bodies from side to side.

Gliders are towed into the air by small planes. Then they are left to fly like a bird on the wind. Can you see the pilot?

Passenger Planes

Big passenger planes carry people from one side of the world to the other. Jumbo jets are the biggest passenger planes. They have very powerful engines and need a long runway to take off.

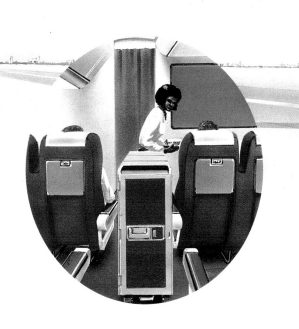

On a long flight, an air steward brings food and drinks on a trolley. The passengers can also watch a film during the flight.

Jumbo jets have
huge wings. This
one has four engines.
How many wheels
can you count?

Concorde is coming in
to land. Can you see its
swept-back wings and
pointed nose? It is the
fastest passenger plane.

On the Ground

This plane has just landed. The airport workers move fast to get the plane ready for take-off again. Trucks wait as the workers unload the baggage, clean the plane and load food for the next flight.

Airport controllers decide when aircraft can take off and land. They use computers and radar to make sure the planes do not fly too close together.

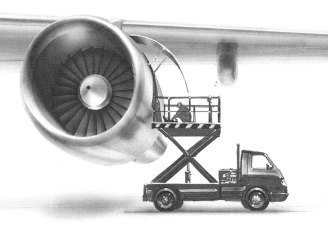

An engineer is lifted up so he can check the huge jet engines.

When the passengers have left the plane, the workers move in. Can you see the truck that pumps fuel from a storage tank under the ground?

Cargo Planes

Some planes carry things rather than people. The nose of this plane lifts up so that the load, called cargo, can be put inside. The cargo is packed into metal boxes called containers. Special trucks lift the heavy containers up to the plane.

The inside of the cargo plane is a big, empty space. Can you see the rails on the floor? The containers slide along the rails on rollers.

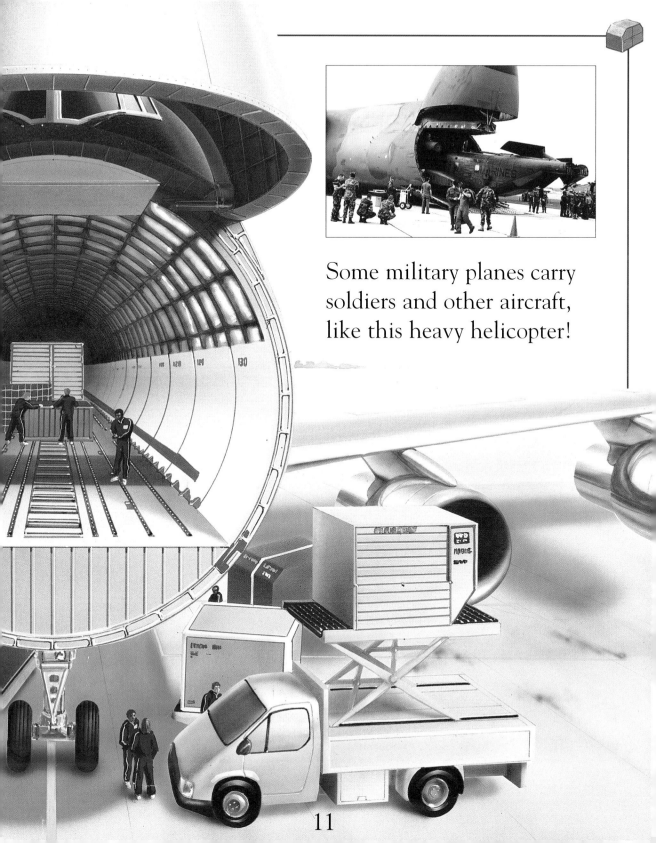

Some military planes carry soldiers and other aircraft, like this heavy helicopter!

Working Hard

Small planes and helicopters do many different jobs. Some planes fight forest fires. First the plane swoops low over a lake or the sea, and scoops water into its tanks.

This small plane looks like a flying insect. It has a glass cockpit so the pilot and crew have a clear view of the ground below. They take photographs that are used to make maps.

This helicopter is fitted with a special sprayer. It sprays the fields with chemicals to kill any insects that might eat the plants.

The pilot then flies over the fire, and presses a switch to open the doors under the plane.

The water pours onto the burning trees. The plane flies back for more water.

Wheeling and Diving

If you go to an air show you might see a team of planes doing circus stunts in the sky. Look how close together these planes are flying. Coloured smoke streams from the engines as they wheel and dive.

This special plane flies upside-down and can loop the loop.

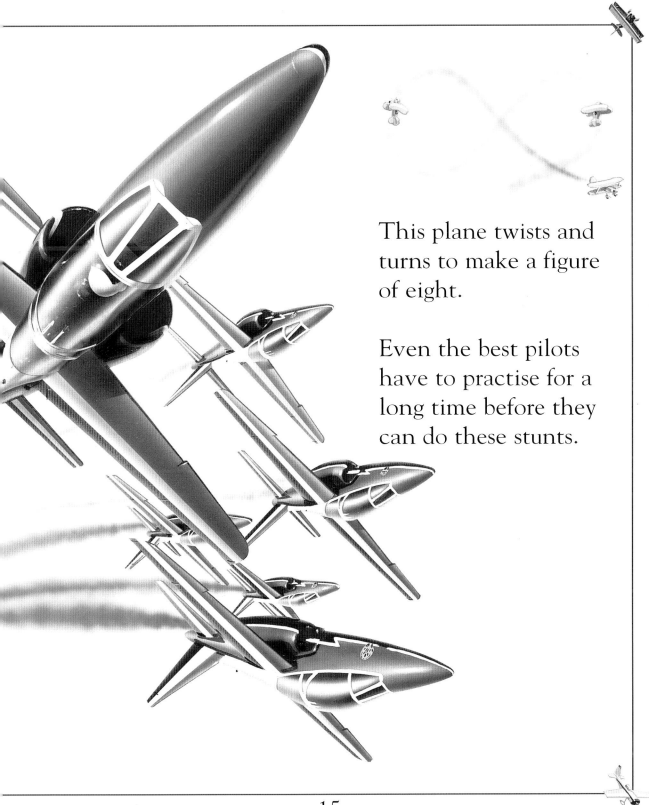

This plane twists and turns to make a figure of eight.

Even the best pilots have to practise for a long time before they can do these stunts.

In the Cockpit

The cockpit is where the pilots sit to fly the plane. Can you see all the controls and computer screens inside the cockpit? They tell the pilot about the plane's height, speed and fuel.

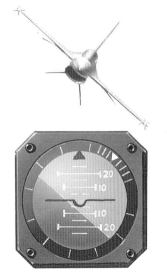

This screen shows whether the plane is flying level to the ground. The white line tilts as the plane turns. Can you see this screen in the cockpit?

The pilot of a warplane may have to get out fast. In an emergency his ejection seat blasts out of the plane and parachutes to the ground.

There are two pilots in a passenger plane – the captain and the co-pilot.

The captain steers the plane with a joystick as it comes in to land on the runway.

Helicopters

A helicopter has long thin blades that spin round. They lift the helicopter into the air and move it up or down, forwards or backwards. Helicopters can hover in the air, and can land on a space as small as a rooftop.

This army helicopter is carrying cargo in nets hanging below it. The nets will make loading and unloading quicker.

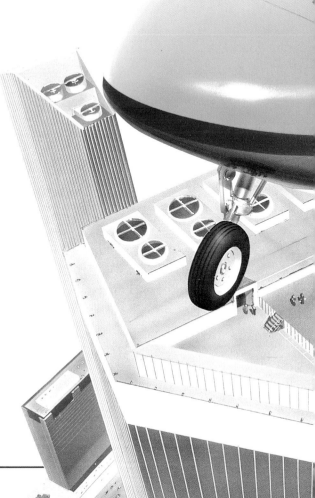

The crew of this helicopter watch for traffic jams in the streets below. They send reports to the radio station, to warn drivers of delays.

Straight Up

Most planes need a long runway to take off, but jump jets can take off from a very small clearing. They can move straight up and down, like a helicopter.

Jump jets are painted special colours and covered with nets so they can be hidden among the trees.

Each jet is flown by a crew of two. How do they get in and out of the jump jet?

Jump jets use gases from the engines to move up and along. Can you see the grey nozzles on each side of the jet, just below the wings?

These nozzles can turn. When they point down, the gases push the jump jet up into the air.

The pilot can make the nozzles point backwards. Now the gases push the jump jet forward.

Warplanes

These warplanes are taking off from a huge ship called an aircraft carrier. The deck is a floating runway. Once the planes are in the air, their wings swing back to make them fly faster.

This strangely shaped warplane is called a Stealth bomber. It has been specially designed so it cannot be detected by radar.

This American fighter plane is over 50 years old. It has a propeller spinning round at the front.

Index

Glossary

Cockpit the part of a plane where the controls needed to fly it are

Crew a team of people who work together on a plane

Hover to stay in the air without moving

Joystick a lever used to steer a plane

Military used by the army, air force or navy

Nose the pointed front of a plane

Nozzle a narrow opening at the end of a jet engine

Parachute a canopy made of silk that slows a person down as he or she falls through the air

Pilot a person that flies a plane

Propeller a set of blades that spin round to move an aircraft forward

Radar an instrument that shows where in the air an aircraft is

Runway a long flat surface where aircraft take off and land

Wheeling changing direction, turning